On Being 20

Aakriti Nandwani

BookLeaf Publishing

India | USA | UK

Presentation by *BookLeaf Publishing*

Web: www.bookleafpub.com

E-mail: info@bookleafpub.com

ISBN:9789358319392

First edition 2023

20

20 is independence,
it is fear,
it is freedom,
it is loss,
it is experiences,
it is an intense loneliness.
The realisation of the true weight of "I miss
you",
the heaviness of "I love you".
20 is a day spent in bed mindlessly watching
Netflix on the phone
with tears streaming from your eyes onto your
arm, seeping into the grey cotton of the t-shirt.
It is a day spent walking around a foreign city
wearing earphones with only the voices of two
strangers to keep you company
while you wander looking for something that
might not even exist, that you don't even know.
It is 24 hours where you do not say a word to
another soul
and when you finally speak your voice is
unsteady and shrill is it echoes through the
phone speaker.
20 is uncertainty.

It is a constant dark and heavy weight in the
lower abdomen,
where the torso meets the legs.
You may forget its existence for a minute or a
day,
even a week, but it is always there and it always
makes itself known,
like a dementor that feeds on you darkest
thoughts and deepest anxieties.
20 is responsibility.
You need to be useful and worthy because who
are you if you don't carry the weight.
Small tasks every day that coalesce into a dark
storm cloud, always hovering above,
threatening to rupture at any moment.
Cloudburst. A deluge of tears breaks through the
dam, immersing the valley,
 rivers cutting their way through a
smooth surface,
trickling down to the
edge, falling for a
long second
and finally seeping into the pages of a book.
20 is failure.
The overwhelming need to get up and work but
you can't lift your head up off the ground,
trapped under an invisible blanket slowly
smothering you,

nothing coming in and absolutely nothing
leaking out.
20 is also dancing alone in your own room
Your favourite songs playing from your phone
And as rush of gratitude warming your bones
Feeling like you are the true version of yourself
for maybe the first time
Feeling lucky just to be alive.

The Wave

Silent, sly the wave sweeps in
The misty dawn
Gently, she caresses exposed feet
Skims along course sand
Sways in and out
Hesitant, wavering,
Unsure if she will stay.
The fog dissipates languidly, taking it's time
And soon enough the wave feels the radiance of
the glowing star on her skin
Warms from the surface down to her core and
begins to glimmer
A thousand tiny jewels glittering through the
surface
Emerald, amethyst, topaz, aquamarine
She decides to stay awhile.

She learns to play with the seagulls ,
Springing up to meet them as they dive down to
tickle her
She explores all the caves and rock pools and
narrows rivulets she finds
When she finds a person, she touches them
gently and changes their decided path
Her essence absorbed into their soul

But sometimes, when she is enraged,
After contracting a scalding poison,
She crashes onto them, bitter and vindictive,
destruction
Blind with fury
Until a rain starts to drizzle,
Then, a cloudburst, a deluge pours in,
Washing away her anger
All that's left is regret and the ability to make
amends.
So she does just that.

After a long day of lilting laughter,
Of tender tears,
Life lived and lives changed,
As the sky darkens into a streak of blazing
orange and twilight blue
She knows it is time to go
And, with a final wave goodbye,
She retreats back into the depths of the ocean,
Yielding her place to her successor,
Gone without a trace,
Except for her handprints on some souls.

A grey hair

I found my first grey hair last year
A silver strand beaming bright against my dark
hair
Like a moonbeam slicing through a dark canopy
I reached up to tear it out but
Stopped
I let it remain

Saw it every day in the mirror as soon as I woke
up
A reminder
I would play with it on my head
Sometimes letting it show like it was a piece of
jewellery
A medal to commemorate my journey
Sometimes pushing it under other strands
Burying the evidence

When I'm being honest, I know
I only left it there because I've heard that if you
pull it out
Another will grow in its place
But I am a liar
So I say it's a statement

Then one day, I pulled a little too hard
Ripped it right out of its ground, unrooted
It was as if a dam had broken and its water
flooded into my veins
Coursing, burning, expanding

Up close the hair was haunting
A glimpse into a colourless future
The flood raged against my hand until I flicked
the hair away and turned on the tap
The flood flushing it down the sink where it
can't hurt me

I wish growing up didn't hurt so much

Anyway
I've decided I'll just be the person that, when it
turns grey
dies her hair crazy colours
Until it's dead

Sounds

The muted sounds of raised voices
Seeping through the cracks in my bedroom door,
Seismic waves to my trembling heart.
I put on my headphones to drown out the noises
but the frayed nerves
Quiver from what the ears cannot feel.

The world narrows down to an erratic thumping,
Speeding up as the deafening whispers draw
near,
Slowing down in the brief moments of quiet,
Laced with venom,
A snake ready to
Annihilate
At the slightest
Provocation.

A simple comment, I wanted to finish the film
we started yesterday.
Tripped over an invisible line, pushed the
hairpin trigger, ruptured the faultline, utter
devastation.
I know I shouldn't blame myself, I am not
responsible.
Words that never settle in me .

I destroyed our peace,
I am too fragile to brave the storm.

Every time the wound develops a scab
We tear it off.
This wound will never heal.
It is stuck between the fights and the fear.
How can someone live like this?

Am I an insensitive bitch for wanting to run.
Be alone.
It is easier to be lonely when you're alone
Than in a crowded room
With ones you love the most.

I am an insensitive bitch.
People fight.
But they're trying and working and all I do is
give up.
I'll be alone forever.
I'm just too fragile,
Or maybe the word is selfish
Growing is pain, changing means losing all the
things you used to be.
I am too scared to let it go,
So, I'll just have to stay alone

The quiet before the next sound
Is the most deafening silence.

It scatters the thoughts in my mind
Until my awareness narrows to the slightest
twitches, the softest sounds,
Warning signs
Before the world erupts,
Before lava seeps through the cracks of the door
I hide behind.

It wraps its arms around me.
I am aflame.
The viscous fluid floods my bloodstream,
Setting my throat ablaze.
I cannot make a sound.
It settles at the bottom of my stomach.
Long after the eruption
I am rooted to the ground,
Weighed down,
While the lava eats through my flesh.

I am left a pile of smoking ashes,
Ready to reform in time for the next eruption.
But before that a handful of ashes drift away in a
Gentle breeze that blows through the open
window,
A piece of the puzzle lost forever.
Maybe it finds another like me somewhere,
Imbeds itself in her skin.
I hope
She does not become like

Me.

The girl in the dress

She lays in bed until 10
but knows she's not lazy
She sits alone in an empty room
but doesn't feel lonely

She goes out every weekend
with all her closest friends
She makes easy demands
without worrying it will all end

She lets her tears fall when she opens her heart
to you,
they leave tracks of mascara behind
She will let you console her with a hug
and not get lost in the maddening maze of her
mind

She buys ice cream whenever she wants
and doesn't have to tear herself to shreds
She twirls in her dress as she appraises herself in
the mirror
but she won't let it fuck with her head

She fights for her beliefs, says exactly what is on
her mind

and yet somehow manages to be the kindest soul
you've ever met
She saved a girl from her father once, did you
know?
She didn't even know her, she's just that perfect.

And even though I don't have close friends, I
hate how I look,
I guard my feelings with a fire-breathing dragon,
while being a coward,
I put one my best dress, stand in front of my
mirror
And I imagine I am her, the most precious
flower.

L'appel du vide

My foot caresses the edge
Of the cliff
A small stone dislodges
Falls
Until I lose track of time
Impossible to hear
But I see a tiny splash
In the water down below
I feel a pull in my chest
A response to the siren's call
Feet glide impossibly closer
To the edge
The end
The feeling grows
Everything fades away
The ice of the wind
The pounding of my heart
The pain
Until there's only me
And the one desire
To jump

Dissolve

15

Because what if I don't want to be me anymore
What if I am tired of this skin
Wouldn't it be sweet
If I were to dissolve into the sky
Fade into a memory
Leave this life behind
A find a new place for me
A place with flowers and lakes and kindness
Where mistakes are forgiven and love is more
than a four letter word
I would dance among the weeds
Bare feet on soft grass
And forget the pain of those broken sobs

And

I toss my phone onto the pillow, a sigh escapes
from my belly
which simmers with a black bile
I push myself off the bed, the creak of the wood
blending in with the croak of my bones
A fuzziness fills my head and I can't gather
enough air to blow it away
I take a step and fall into my swivel chair
I open my laptop and open a browser with 47
tabs open
One of only 6

My mouth feels dry so I want to drink some
water
Except my water bottle is empty
So I should go downstairs and fill it
But I don't have time
I have to start on this assignment, which is due
in 4 hours
and then I have another, which I haven't started
yet, obviously
and I have to reply to four emails
and apply to six new jobs
and I have to spend time with my family so that
they don't feel like I am neglecting them even

though i know they are probably fine and I'm the
one that craves their company
and I should probably make lunch because
Mummy is busy with work
and I have to start watching that new show
and I promised myself I would start reading
again like I did when I was eleven
and I need to figure out how to make friends
and, while I'm at it, how to fall in love so that I
don't die alone
and I have to decide what I want to do with my
life
and start going to the gym again
and find a hobby to enjoy when I'm old and don't
have anything to do or anyone to talk to
and I don't even understand why I can't just
write this essay when philosophy was always my
favourite
and...

Nature

Streaks of orange and crimson light the world
aglow
The ground before my feet undulates with the
whispers of wind
Glittering like precious jewels
The sight pierces my skin like pinpricks ,
finding a home inside,
dazzling,
humbling

Without the rasping raven song, without the
croaking crickets,
Without the rays of light, lilting melody
Of streams and soft silence of a starry night
How would we ever find beauty
And love
Truth

The ticking of a clock has no
Meaning, if not for the birth
And death
Of each new day.

Chocolate

The warmth in the heavy air
Threatens my entire existence.
I can feel my form giving up,
Little by little,
And I know the end is approaching.
My every nightmare is coming to
Fruition.
My only hope is that I am consumed before I
dissolve
Completely.
A peaceful death after fulfilling my
Purpose.
I melt like a piece of chocolate on a sweltering
day,
Formless,
Slowly… and then in an instant.
The sun continues to heat up the small room,
Like a fire in a furnace,
Cooking clay pots.
But instead of making me stronger,
Eternal,
The heat continues to weaken my strength,
The pressure splinters me into a million tiny
fractures,
And, with a last gasp

For untouchable cool air,
I fall,
A messy puddle on a clean table.

Trouble

Double Double
Toil and trouble
The fire burns
The cauldron bubbles

The eyes of fate show rubble
Venomous fluid pours in

Simmer down in a bed of ice
Swap the fire for another vice
Numb the feelings, awash with liquid nitrogen
Don't let them vie for another slice

They claw and tear at your skin
Until you're stained/glow with blood red ink
But you must conceal your scars
From those you love with a tearful rinse

Confetti

When two people love each other completely,
the rest is
Confetti
Some harsh and heavy pieces
Overbearing/overwhelming
Getting into the eyes
Causing salt water to flow in streams
Down
The
Face
And crashing into the skin with startling force
They stick (until they're shaken off)

Some are
Light
And
Glittery
Adding a sparkle to a thoroughly illuminated
world
They sit in the hair and upon the face
So light they cannot be felt
But enhance their beauty for the world to admire

When two people are in love, the world is a
Celebration

Honouring the sacred connection between two
souls

Legendary Conflicts

I used to see you an armlength away
Close enough to touch
Only I would notice your rare, fleeting smiles
I loved you so much

Your eyes held a constellation of shooting stars,
A new world for me to see
I placed my life in your outstretched hand
Gravity lost its power over me

Your sharp gaze betrayed a glimpse of your soul
And stole my heart away
So now I lie, waves of misery lapping at my
shores
An empty shell I stay

Because these legendary conflicts lead to
Legendary heartaches
Leaving you shattered and unscrewed
Wishing it had all been fake

Like a nuclear bomb explosion, debris flies
every way,
A cloud blocks out the sky

Wandering the deserted street, I breathe in the
acid rain
Force myself to say goodbye

But even when the dust settles, the clouds part
Birds sing, people move on
I cannot exorcise your ghost from my bones
I cannot stop singing our song

Years later that poison still burns through my
veins
Corroding my soul, replacing it with ire
Just another victim who stood too close to the
flame
And lost themselves to the fire.

Because these legendary conflicts lead to
Legendary heartaches
Knowing the most beautiful, true thing you ever
did
Was your worst mistake

They say memories fade, bodies decay
From dust we emerge, to dust we'll return
But I know loving you is a catastrophe
That can never be undone

Because these legendary conflicts lead to
Legendary heartaches

And legendary love stories always end in
Violent heartbreaks

26

Shooting Star

Ending is the love letter sitting
untouched
within the pages of my favourite book, which I
gave you that you never cared enough to
read.

Ending is the way I always shout across
the void,
not so loud that you are disturbed,
and you take a day just to wave back to
me.

I understand, or at least I try, your world is
so much fuller
than me, and you have no need to
continue to water this
seed.

Yet, I hope one day you'll find that letter
somehow,
maybe when the book falls
to the floor as you
clean.

You'll understand that, even though we were a
fleeting
spark
of feeling in this never-stopping
grinding, crushing, cutting
machine.

I will never forget that you give my
life meaning
despite not being in it, despite being
a shooting star, I will hold on to you like a sweet
dream.

Maybe you will miss me, just for a
transient moment,
and find yourself writing a note for me
to discover when I turn my letterbox
key.

On loneliness

There's something about the loneliness I feel in a
car
Confined in the smallest space with everyone
I love
And no one cares
The tears leaking out
Of control
While I try to hide the evidence
Shield my face with a cloak of hair
And an armour made of my quiet stillness
While my mind rages with irrepressible thoughts
Who do you think you are?
You don't get to judge
Be disappointed
At your failure
That you think is me
But it is really just yourself
You failed yourself yet you take it out on me
As if cutting yourself open for me
Makes me a puppet
For you to mould into what you could never be
When you will never know what it fells like to
be caged in these bones
So carelessly
You shattered a piece of me

That I watered and grew with my love for you
It is a cruel condition
To be trapped here
In a car with the subject of my hurt
As we speed off down the highway
And still I love you
You cut yourself open for me

Fear

He comes
He stands between my life and my death
He feeds on uncertainty
The unknown
His weakness is knowledge, experience
So he fights against it,
Holds me back
He makes me weak,
Inconsiderate
Cruel
Selfish
Safe
He hinders understanding
Possibility
Extravagance
He filters the images
Entering my eyes
Until they are not
Red and blue and green
But grey, and then
He causes the grey to bleed
From my greyscale world
Until I only see in black and white

Patchwork Quilt

I inherited my hair from you.
It curls the same way
And greys the same way
And when you lean your head against mine
I feel it blending and dissolving into yours
Taking me with it.

Your love is the remaining warmth from your feet
Leeching into my skin,
Warming me from my soul to the tips of my toes
After you see me standing
Bare feet on cold stone tiles in the middle of winter
And you give me the skippers you were wearing
So I wouldn't suffer the cold.

You wear a bindi
And tell me it's to hide the crease in your forehead,
A valley eroded into the surface of your skin.
I think there's no need to hide it.
When I'm perplexed or perturbed,
Worried or wondering,
That same line appears on my skin too

Like an engraving etched into stone.
The more I live, the more I learn
That carving will become deeper, permanent
Until It's just like yours.

My earliest memory is of playing with you,
Dressing up in your saree,
Royal red, bride of laughter.
You would drench me in gold,
Necklaces, earrings, bangles
Then take countless pictures.

I didn't understand then, but now,
When I wear your saree,
I feel the weight,
The tale of
Your history becoming mine.
A legacy is born.

A multicoloured, incandescent, opalescent orb
blooms in my chest
When you hand me my gift,
A picture book about me as Katniss Everdeen
With pictures you drew and words you wrote.
I have never felt so known
As when you know me.

The only time I get to hold your hand now

Is when we arm wrestle on the empty dining
room table.
You always win and still I want to go again and
again,
Because I've never felt so strong as when your
hand pushes mine to the wood
And you grin with glee of victory.
I hope my hand does the same for you.

I am not me when I am made up of so much of
you.
I am a patchwork quilt
Stitched together with fragments of all of you
And threads of my essence.

Seasons

Bright, soft sunlight illuminates the picture
Wildflowers and weeds bloom and billow in a
brilliant array
Every shade, feelings of a young heart
Drops of elixir from the sky that holds me in its
arms
Ambrosia for the newly planted seeds
In a fertile ground
It is a time for frolicking and falling
Loving and learning
Dancing and despair

The soft sunlight gives way to a ruthless
radiance
 The breeze thickens and settles
A viscous poison
It is a grinding labour to struggle through the
haze
But it is important to work
To tend to the crops growing, unhurried
And those moments when I make it to the beach
And waves of cool, clear water wash over my
feet
Or
Sleepless nights where the stars seem to

Dance, glimmer, shimmer just for me
Everything become worthwhile

The dense cloud lifts as the temperature falls
The leaves too
Blanket the soil in burnt umber, flaming orange
and aged maroon
Hopeless yet hopeful
Pain and beauty
The harvest is ready to reap
Ripe and sweet with history
A medal commemorating the arduous journey I
took to get this far

My harvest comes in use finally
When the cold comes
I survive the barrenness for a little while until
A blizzard blows in and envelopes
Envelopes me in its
Embrace.
All I see is a cloud of iridescent white
I smile
I am absorbed
The storm rages for a few short moments
And then
I am gone